From the Dust

From the Dust

SARAH JANE LEVIN

to Gibson,
for teaching me
that we can be
loving and broken,
kind and fearful,
yet still be perfect.

CONTENTS

THE WORLD 11

THE MISTAKES 47

THE PEOPLE 73

THE ADVICE 101

INTRODUCTION

While it's difficult to notice through the noise (and dust) sometimes, in fact, there are exceptional people. More than a few, to be sure. Some are hard workers, some are thoughtful, some are well organized, some shine. This collection of poems shows Jane Levin to have all of those qualities and more.

From the Dust is an experience. A journey from middle school to young adult, it's a glimpse inside the heart and soul of growth. The heartache, the headbands, the hopes and dreams and disappointments. There is love and wonder. There is realization. All of the lessons of a life lived, whether thoughtfully or with abandon.

And there is beauty and affinity in the language. Jane sinks through the "floors of my stomach" and finds her place amid the "stars of my sky." She notices and appreciates that her imagination "decided to stick around" and she embodies the idea that "lights are meant to shine."

From the Dust is a reflection on Jane's relationships; with the world, with herself, with the people around her, with her own flourishing mind and spirit.

It's beautiful.

David Levin
Cortlandt Manor, NY
July 2020

THE WORLD

I've learned a lot about feelings in the past few years. I've discovered people who define their moon and their stars as a simple feeling inside of their head. I've been taught how to love, especially when it's hard. I've experienced neglect, rejection, selfishness, toxicity, and simple indifference. All of these feelings have brought me to a place of clarity I had never imagined before. I can look ahead and see clouds of fog and shadow, but absolutely nothing about the dark clouds scares me away anymore. If anything, the small bit of fear is stemming from my very own desire to be different, to be extraordinary. I know you've seen it in movies, the people who beg to live their lives as a unique soul. Don't you feel it, though? Can't you see the appeal of the snow white daisy in a sea of red roses? The fog and shadows practically push me forward, itching for something new. Anything new. If I've learned anything thus far, it's that something better can always come. Someone new can step right in when all of your so-called people decide that they simply cannot see you anymore. Something new can step right in when you can't stand the view anymore. I've been told of my energy my whole life. It's been loved, it's been despised, and it's been ignored. I won't let any of those opinions guide me anymore, for the tempting dark clouds and fog through the trees are more than enough for me now.
- s.j.l.

I'm up in the twinkles
I'm down in cement

I'm right to go further
I'm left to stay bent

I'm light when I exhale
I'm dark when I sigh

I'm happy I knew them
I'm sad to say goodbye
- s.j.l.

You've inhaled it with grace, truly breathed it in,
and exhaled it all back out into the earth.
You've grabbed it with every ounce of energy inside of you,
wrapped it around your soul,
and shoved it back out into the universe.
You've mournfully swallowed it,
allowed yourself to taste its every bite,
and left it there to hollow out that solemn yet loving place
you had always found yourself escaping to.
Not once, though, have you left it there
to wallow in itself.
The responsibility has always been yours.
The days and nights and sun and moon
have found themselves coming back around again,
all the same.
And while you're doing it differently each time,
everyone else thinks it is all the same.
- s.j.l.

Haven't you stripped the weeds of your garden?
Where are the blossoms of those who haven't seen the world yet?
How many dead plants have you been watering?
How many have you pulled?
- s.j.l.

I sew through the holes of a button
to make my jacket a bit more snug.
It fits a bit warmer now.
It looks a bit stronger now.
It works all the same.

I sew through the pockets of my jeans
to make them a bit more uncommon.
They look a bit cheerful now.
They act a bit trendy now.
They fit all the same.

I sew a patch over my heart
to make the mourning of you a bit more bearable.
You are a bit further now.
You look a bit different now.
You feel all the same.
- s.j.l.

Something ethereal is
by definition
too delicate for this world.
Are my memories
of you
not in the world
anymore?
- s.j.l.

I hope I dance
when the floor is too sweltering
and my feet can't stand
to stay perfectly still.

I hope I dance
when the drought of my riches
comes in the form
of smiles and beams.

I hope I dance
to remind myself
of the ones I will always have
because they danced
with me.
- s.j.l.

You stood right next to me
but my soul was much further away
you see
I felt solar systems
away from you
yet all I could do was stay.
- s.j.l.

There is something about
the sound of the birds in the morning
to reassure me that a new day
means a new mind.

There is something about
the smell of the air in the morning
to remind me that the sun
is back and brighter now.

There is something about
the sight of my dogs in the morning
to show me that their smiles
should reflect back on my face.

There is something about
the taste of fruit in the morning
to recount my gratitude, mom
for its intentional placement on the plate.
- s.j.l.

I've found myself losing sleep, but it's been okay.
It's been the music that should be making me drowsy.
Rather,
I've found myself wanting to stay awake just to hear the end of the song.
- s.j.l.

When I was eight years old I asked for a chandelier for my birthday.
All of the princess tales and charming fantasies just had me enchanted.
It hung right over my head
as I leaped over the stepping stones of my youth.
My first sentiments of infatuation, comfort, and agony.
The pink pillows on my bed
got awfully used to being squeezed for solace.
If only my walls could speak.
If only I had just looked up.
The chandelier of my hopelessly beautiful daydreams
was always right there above me.
- s.j.l.

Like some sort of
forsaken fidelity
of the moon,
the stars
stretched their distance.
- s.j.l.

Let yourself climb disquieting, uninterrupted mountains.
Feel yourself surrender
to the perfectly painted canvas of a view.

The colorful leaves
that beg to show their
lonely faces.

The perfect sunset
that captures
everything you ever imagined
in yourself.

The eloquent
yet terribly
wordless
definition of beauty
that you hide
beneath your cabinets and shelves
filled with acceptance.

They tell you to enjoy the view
- s.j.l.

I have seldom felt like a puppet
but this time I move my own strings
I seek and plead to cut them off
and turn them into wings.
- s.j.l.

Sitting there as the sun dimmed, staring back into our soul-searched hearts, I could feel the gratitude almost dripping from the balcony. Taking in one of the most beautiful places I had ever been with one of the most beautiful souls I had ever met. The sunset reflected off the twinkling water as it effortlessly flowed through the canals of the city. The crowds were getting smaller and the streets were getting quieter. We watched the entire city fall asleep, we watched the entire sky as it concluded its beautiful, 24-hour light show. If our minds could actually take snapshots of all the moments we craved to never forget, this moment would be at the very top of the stack of photographs. Part of me felt as if it was almost too good to be true. For just a second, we both could stare back at the changing colors of the sky and feel so very small.

You grow up being told that you are anything but small, that your words and experiences are meant to be heard and seen. Yet looking up at the sky and past the world, looking through all of the stars and planets and galaxies, we felt so small but so content. There is this entire atmosphere above us, and we aren't even sure how much of the vastness is unknown. So instead of letting it scare us, we looked past all of the sadness and trauma and fear of our lives and our minds, and everything felt so still. I wanted nothing but to sit in those chairs until the water had nothing else left to reflect and the streets had no more bicyclists to carry. If moments could be paused, I would have made this one last forever.

Amsterdam
- s.j.l.

If only
the dandelions
stuck between my toes
could stick around
and let the wind
take them to a hundred
different
places
like I will.
- s.j.l.

We are so concerned with the way that everything seems to look.
We abuse the power of the mirror,
and let it eat parts of us that are naturally supposed to remain untouched.
What can you see?
What can be absorbed like the mirrors do?
Where is the perspective in looking down at things from such a
heightened bird's-eye view?

I want to be absolutely certain
that the people cradled in the stars can see all of the good.
I want to hear the glistening of smiles and the deep ringing of tears
when I stare up into the unknown.
Nothing is as comfortable as the sky,
a blanket of familiarity for the world can truly be so small.

A letter to the sky
- s.j.l.

I accidentally found something good
one day.
I picked it from the ground
and held it up to my eyes
in the wind.
Like serendipity
it was unexpected
but it was
splendid.
- s.j.l.

Soulmate
is a confusing word to me
because shouldn't my soul
be okay by itself
and shouldn't the others
survive the mountains
without needing
a walking stick
- s.j.l.

They say home is where the heart is,
but my heart is all over the world.

It is stuffed in a bookshelf
of a bookstore in Paris
and dancing on trees with monkeys
in the cloud forest of Costa Rica.

It is brushed onto a painting of broccoli
in the streets of London
and swimming with ducks
in a fountain in Spain.

It is perched atop a white building
in the islands of Greece
and overlooking the view
from a restaurant in Italy.

It is basking in the sun
on the beaches of Israel
and floating down a river
through the quaint towns of Germany.

It is snorkeling with fish
in the waters of Bermuda
and looking up at the castles
in the center of Prague.

It is hiking the mountains
of the Galapagos Islands
and roaming with animals
on the peaceful fields of Ireland.

It is biking through the streets
splitting the canals of Amsterdam
and almost getting arrested on a tram
in the city of Berlin.

They say home is where the heart is,
but my heart is all over the world.
Calling the world my home seems
impossible
but let's prove them wrong.
- s.j.l.

I've brought myself straight to the sea,
I've dragged myself beneath a tree.
I've watched the dreams and fears unfold,
I've sat atop this world of gold.

She's taught me all I've ever known,
She's given me strength in the form of stone.
She's let me guide my own two feet,
She's left my novel of knowledge complete.
- s.j.l.

As if the perfect city could not exist,
you found yourself feeling at home
thousands of miles away.
The waves found themselves
crashing atop tradition, comfort,
and wonderful ritual.
And you shuffled your way into
years of these perfect indulgences.
The beaches of tribes under the sun
carried you
to the flashing lights beneath the moon.
It was the ultimate mixture of friendliness
yet a new world unexplored.

And you were happy.
- s.j.l.

So many people have come and gone,
they never knew each other
but they all knew me
and maybe by now
they have met in my heart
and seen their likeness
but their disparities too.
- s.j.l.

I used to watch the tree outside my window as if it were a friend.
I'd wish it a good morning and tell it about my day.
I'd cry as I imagined myself counting the rings
inside of its restless, robust bones.
It's different now.
It's still a friend.
I'm not speaking to it anymore.
As everything lies still, I'm not picturing the rings
beneath its sturdy structure.
Instead, I'm counting them inside of me and inside of others.
As if each ring represents a piece of the tree that I took away,
or a piece of the friendship I had lost to someone else.
Where are all of the rings now?
Off dreaming up their own fantasies,
leaving me helplessly trapped in their jumbled minds?
Where is the tree now?
Right outside staring back at me.
Even though there's no self portrait taped up staring back.
- s.j.l.

The bridge
that used to be ours
is now filled with being
and I can't help but wish
that my feet could stick out
of the sides of your car
and my hair could sweep
straight in front of my eyes
and my mind could be empty
of shadows.
- s.j.l.

If only the leaves could speak behind their screen,
to tell us exactly the things they have seen.

Whether it be the thawing of layers of ice and stone,
or the budding of the ground beneath their roots and bones.

The leaves have seen more than we could ever intend,
and the concept of patience seems something to befriend.
- s.j.l.

Whenever I'm listening to a song, I like to imagine the ideal place,
person, time, and situation where it would be perfect
background noise.
I envision it for happy songs, sad songs,
and every single one in between.
I find it quite comforting, as I'm able to make up an entire
circumstance in my head for a simple set of lyrics and chords.
I believe that there is a certain spectrum when it comes to songs, too.
I imagine ones that are a bit too sad as me having the best company
in the world, sitting on my driveway with a blanket
and staring up at the stars.
The ones that have enough sadness to bear alone are those which I
imagine myself at 1am, driving home from a friend's house
and blasting the music with the windows down, remaining the
perfect amount of chilly because I've got a sweatshirt on.
I've found that while everyone else's imagination seemed to run
away by the time we reached middle school,
mine decided to stick around.
I talk to myself constantly.
Holding a narrative in my head all day,
as if I've got some sort of an audience.
I picture certain situations that would change my behavior
or attitude towards such basic activities.

When I want to take a quick shower, I imagine that I have a fancy event later that night that I'm rushing to get ready for, or I think about having the most perfect person waiting for me right outside in the next room.
If I want to sit outside and bask in the sun for a few minutes, I imagine myself to be famished of simple rays of sun, letting them shine onto my face as if I hadn't seen the light in days.
The simple fact that I tend to listen to music a bit too much makes my life seem more imaginative than real.
I am waiting for people in instances that have never yet seemed to happen, but at least I'm imagining a world different from this one, right?

My Imagination
- s.j.l.

The picnic blanket was filled
with rich, plentiful fruits
that we begged to consume
on the side of laughter,
conversation,
and simple human touch.
- s.j.l.

The Japanese maple tree seems to have a few of its own definitions of beauty.
I used to watch as its pink flowers blossomed into darker, stronger leaves of red.
- s.j.l.

I'm not scared of the dresser in my dining room anymore.
I'm not scared of the gargoyles in my fairytale books.
Or the reflection from the lights outside of my front door.

I'm scared of the pits in the floors of my stomach.
I'm scared of getting close to people
because they always seem to find a way to leave.
I'm scared of boys whose names begin with T.

The dresser in the dining room
and the fairytale gargoyles
and the way the light reflects on the front door
seems almost tranquilizing to me now.
- s.j.l.

Don't you want to know
if the stars of my sky
have found a place to stay?
- s.j.l.

THE MISTAKES

Forgiveness seems easy
when you've become an expert at smiling.
As if a smile speaks wonders,
as it echoes into their mind
as something other than
a desperate cry for help.
You can tuck it far away,
behind a corner somewhere,
but it'll always be
in the back of your mind.
How they couldn't even salvage an apology
because the entire earth, moon, and sun
seemed to revolve right around their finger.
How your presence in a room
isn't even physical anymore.
How you thought that these were the people
who would be there.
Life is funny that way, right?
I like to say it just keeps me on my toes.
Onto the next adventure, the next trip, the next fresh start.
This time will be different, but haven't you heard that before?
May your secrets in your hidden corners
beg to show their beautiful faces,
and may your smiles become a bit more real.
- s.j.l.

I was the train tracks
you were the train
but you need clouds in the sky
if you're asking for rain.
- s.j.l.

Looking back on it all,
all of the laughing and crying and learning and growing,
I always come back to one thing.
As if those drives in the dark
blasting the songs you know will make you cry
could do anything at all.
And you say they're different,
and how could they compare,
but you are left the same way every single time.
And maybe a small piece of you has changed,
for him or for you.
But you're left every time in your car
with the windows down,
blasting those tear-inducing songs,
desperately trying to feel something.
- s.j.l.

Hollowed bookshelves
Empty chapters
Crowded words
- s.j.l.

Someone told me once
that the opposite of love
is indifference
and not hate.
So is the opposite of happiness
detachment
and not sadness?
Is the opposite of you
distance
and not someone new?
- s.j.l.

I am done apologizing
for the puddles you have stepped in
from the rainstorm I couldn't control.

I am tired of begging
for a single piece of a star
when your entire sky
is luminous with liars.

I am dreading the day
when you swarm back for mending
because I have hidden my sewing kit
in the back of the closet

but would take it back out
for you
again.
- s.j.l.

I thought the meditations and vinyasa flows
could rid the unlucky notions
and the unfavored memories
but I have learned that those are just part of me
and that the meditations and vinyasa flows
should let me approach them
handle them
welcome them
for they are a part of me
and there they must remain.
- s.j.l.

Our whole being then becomes
the flaws that we point out in the mirror.
We are solely the imperfections of ourselves.
- s.j.l.

If we had just let ourselves stay in the water
a little bit longer
and let our hearts marinate
in the spontaneity,
really soaked our souls in it,
all of our daring escapades
would have meant so much more
to me now.
- s.j.l.

He told you he wanted every day to be special for you.
He told you he could see himself squeezing your hand
for much longer than he ever thought he would admit.
He made sure you knew that he'd never break your heart.
As if you weren't surprised,
you found yourself drowning in tears and deep,
hollow pits in your stomach while the simple moon lit the sky.
He threw it all behind him and went running.
No part of him seemed to care or to question.
And each day, the squeezes became more faint in the back of your mind.
You tried to be okay, you managed to be okay.
But now it's all new.
And now he isn't there to lay his head on your shoulder on the airplane
or to play with your hair as you cry yourself to sleep on his chest.
You're doing it all by yourself now,
and you promised that you'd be stronger this time.
- s.j.l.

Interference is funny if it is embellished with gold
around a perfect portrait of the exact person that comes to mind.
While the empty frames scream into the void
of those who we thought would be there.
And with interference comes a desire to be different.
A desire to hang up the perfect portrait,
just a bit more extraordinary than the next.
And we stare straight ahead, hopelessly trying to find any sign at all.
- s.j.l.

I think of you.
I think of your arms,
wrapped around the corners of my ribs,
as we laid there,
remarkably still and content,
for hours.
The uncertainty yet
overwhelming feeling of comfort
left me wishing
that moments could have a pause button.
If it was the city,
the mindset,
the situation,
or simply the euphoria left in our bones,
we can't say we'll ever know.
And yet,
part of me is killing
for the comfort again
while also not wanting to feel anything at all.
- s.j.l.

We held buttercups up to our chins
in hopes of a reflection
other than the shimmers
of its yellow petals.
- s.j.l.

Loving someone is a lot more
than just butterflies in your stomach
and the skipping of a beat within your heart.
Loving someone requires a piece of you,
a part of this soul that has been through
more than you could ever try to scribble down
with a pen and paper.
It's about the nights
when you want nothing else
but to be alone,
the days when you find
that you're keeping yourself busy
just to avoid looking down
at your phone.
Is it their fault
or is it yours?
Can you stop loving somebody
that easily?
Like the dirt on your windshield,
you can just wipe them away.
When did they become
so easily replaceable?
Or if you're not like me,
when did they become so easily
removable?
- s.j.l.

If only she knew just how to separate the walls put up to keep the ghosts of those she thought she once knew from trying to prove themselves yet again.
- s.j.l.

What a shame it would be
to let the simple words
of one innocent stranger
keep us from sharing
french onion soup
ever again.
- s.j.l.

Bringing yourself to a sense of clarity
seems like the perfect idea
until it overwhelms your subconscious
with the hidden fears of your spirit.
Those daydreams filled with
remarkably
exhilarating
desires
can't find their spot next to the
simplicity
of it all.
They tell you that shouldn't stop you,
that you are built of
so
much
more
than the impossibility of a dream.
Do you believe them all?

What comes to mind
when they ask if you believe?
Are you believing their demands
or are you believing
in the dreams themselves?
That's the ultimate distinction
of ambition beneath the
hidden fears.
What you choose to do with them
reveals everything.
- s.j.l.

Like a cup of tea
I filled up to the brim
piping hot water
of spaces within.
- s.j.l.

I often found myself seeing things as "just enough."

Wouldn't "enough" look different
if it were engraved with your name?

Wouldn't "enough" be stronger
if it were encouraged by your words?

Wouldn't "enough" look taller
if it were submerged in your confidence?

Wouldn't "enough" be enough
if I could just let you go?
- s.j.l.

We will never be anything
but the shattered glass
after it hits against the floors
simply made for breaking.
And we will break
as if we were only built
with the weakest parts.
As if anything a bit strong
could simply fracture
our already broken bones.

And we will lie motionless
for we will never be
the same
again.
- s.j.l.

Like a light switch
I thought
I could simply
turn off
these feelings
and watch them
flicker away.
- s.j.l.

I often find myself buried beneath a sense
of longing for what has been stripped away.
As if clutching a necklace between my fingertips
could bring me thousands of miles away.
- s.j.l.

Like a tear in the fabric of time
I pulled apart the threads of you
from my newly worn sweater
and shoved it in the back of my drawer.

It should have stung a bit more than it did
because I have been struggling
to rip you from my reflection in the mirror
for too long now.

Taking the sweater off
kept it out of the reflection
but staring into my own eyes
I could see you right back
like no time had passed
at all.
- s.j.l.

THE PEOPLE

It feels like the words are infinite
but so is the construct of time.
You are my poem and you are my person.
However long,
it is worth the climb.
- s.j.l.

I do not care for coffee
especially when it is strong.
I do not wish for love now
unless it can be temporary.

I do not worry for my brother
because he has seen too many movies
with superheroes.

I do not dream of former fantasies
since they are not real
and life's breaks and tears
cannot be portrayed
in the little daydreams
of mine.
- s.j.l.

You think you've seen it all, heard it all, experienced it all.
Taken it with the same energy as the time before
and stomped on it like a crunchy, fallen leaf
on your driveway.
Sixteen-year-old you, watching from afar,
as he sits on the pavement with you years later,
wrapped around a blanket and staring up at the stars,
like you had done so many times before.
There's something different about this time.
There's something strange about all of those
white picket fence fantasies.
And it's not a bad thing,
maybe even not a good thing either.
It just sits with you, settles in your jam-packed mind,
squeezes itself right into your thoughts.
The gears shift an entire year in advance.
Heartbroken you, saying goodbye to another,
as if it's really a goodbye to last forever.
The spontaneous, weekend-long segments
of what you actually thought meant happiness
couldn't do it for you anymore.
Yet another old sweatshirt that you couldn't stand
to keep in the back of your closet.

And you thought that was it.
That the long drawn breaths of supposed sadness
were enough for your jam-packed mind.
But yet another version of your so-called falling leaves
paused your so-called wisdom.
Right on schedule, too.
This one's different.
Heard that before?
And you think the leaves have fallen
and you've walked right over them,
but they're taking their sweet time,
he's taking his deep breaths,
and you're taking it all in.
How you've learned so much from that simple word
that everyone claims to know so well.
Love seems like the right one,
but it's starting to feel a bit more like
a simple sense of comfort
with every bite of it you take.
And you think you've seen it all,
but don't new leaves fall down every October?
And the shoes you're wearing, they change too.
- s.j.l.

I've always liked to drink tea.
I would add honey,
always too much.
I would offer it to you
when you didn't feel well.
I would make you some
and bring it out to your car.
Oh what I'd do
to be able to make you tea
one more time.
- s.j.l.

A friend becomes more than a friend
when they have shared the stage with you,
when you have cried for the same endings,
when they have applauded your debuts.

Nine friends become more than a clique
when they can recite your own growth better than you can,
when time with them is easy and filled with relief.
When they can distract you from the noise and the clouds,
when the laughs in the middle of the night
are more than just
bowls of spaghetti.
- s.j.l.

Like my dog
resting his heavy head on my lap
and watching his chest rise and fall in a sigh,
I crave the feeling of letting go.
Like his excitement
for any stranger to approach our door,
I understand his feeling of welcoming new friends.

I wish I could tell him
that everything he feels
is simply a pebble
to the boulder seen
falling
through the
mountains
of being.
- s.j.l.

You told me once
that if I held up eleven daisies
and stared in a mirror,
I would be looking at
the twelve most beautiful things
in the world.

It has rung in my ears to this day,
to think that someone has seen me
to be something
just as beautiful
as what my mother considers
the happiest flower
on earth.
- s.j.l.

In the market right in the center of the city,
alive with the simple desire for chirpy interaction,
live some olives with the pits inside.

And we'd laugh as we watched
the old, clever man
fill our ten-shekel container
of pitless olives.

And we crave the interaction
in the perfect place
more than we ever thought we could.

Hell, we'd even try an olive with the pit inside for it.
- s.j.l.

Always remain independent, but be sure to have a safety net.
Having a few diamonds is more valuable than having too many stones.
Let people walk in and out of your life and handle it with grace.
Stay high, and stay happy. It's just like praising the dogs.
Keep your insecurities present, but embrace them.
They are beautiful that way.
Take in as much of nature as you can.
It is there to be seen.
You are here to be seen.
You are beautiful this way.

Advice my mom never realized she was giving me
- s.j.l.

I don't think I ever told you
that my grandpa taught me
about purpose.
I don't think you know
that he sat outside for hours
as I leaped into the pool
in hopes of his ranking
to be higher than an eight.
I don't think I ever shared with you
the long conversations we had
about my life and prosperous future.
And I know I never told you
that he is my catalyst
to this day
for my triumph
and my growth.
- s.j.l.

If only the bits of flour on her fingertips
could speak for everything inside of her crowded mind.

She doesn't wash them off,
in hopes that their utter presence will remind her
of the things she left unsaid.

Instead, she bakes a cake.
- s.j.l.

That's the thing about guys we can't trust.
They'll tempt you and tell you that their feelings are simply
a mystery waiting to be cracked.
Aren't you scared?
That's the fun.
We all say it, and we all believe it.
Until it's not a mystery anymore.
It may have only taken weeks, but it may have taken years.
It may fill you with ambiguity, but it may build you with hope.
And it all crashes down once it's over.
Once the mystery is really, really solved.
Aren't you alone, enough of a mystery?
Can't your own soul be the special thing to crack?
Yet we find this strange comfort in the ambiguity of others.
Something we can't truly ever get back.
That's the thing about girls who won't look inside of themselves.
- s.j.l.

Like a pebble in my shoe
I wish I could
hang on and roam the world with you
for just a little bit longer.
- s.j.l.

*When the simple urge of protection is all that you can muster up,
while feeling overwhelmed by the mere abandonment
of the very person you were trying to protect.*

When the sudden urge of fulfillment rang through your ears,
as you wrung your brain free of the old friends,
because this one was real
and this one had no end.

When you were proven uninformed yet again,
as you wanted nothing but the end of this dreadful day,
and you found yourself asking
isn't anyone going to stay?
- s.j.l.

Someone will always see us as the empty halls and dusty furniture.
Empty halls that are forgotten, dusty furniture that is broken and used.
Someone will always see us as the closed doors and winding staircases.
Doors closed so long they are stuck,
winding staircases so long they are tiresome.
Someone will always see us as forgotten, broken, used, and tired.
But that doesn't stop us.
- s.j.l.

An Egyptian princess once told me
that everything happens for a reason.
That every rainstorm acts as a screen of vapor
to blind us of the truth.
She tells me the truth.
She says, "As you run through the crowded columns
of built up memories and fantasies,
I will be there."
I will stand as you remember it all.
I will wrap you in my arms
and fill you with warmth when you crumble.
I will keep you safe, but not too safe.
You have things to experience, too.

I once told an Egyptian princess
that everything happens for a reason.
That the difficulty to breathe
and the emptiness in your chest
is there to remind you of something.
I tell her that something.
I say, "As you inhale the pure whisps of new imagination,
you exhale what once was."
What once battled your darker clouds.
What once gave you a fresh sensation of belonging.
What once let you stand out
amongst a field of white daisies.
You have things to learn, too.
- s.j.l.

How are you?
How is your family?
Is your father feeling better?
Can you take a deep breath for me?
Doesn't it all feel a bit too heavy sometimes?
Where are your fears now?
When do you feel the most safe?
Call ended.

All of the things I'd ask but wouldn't say.
- s.j.l.

She didn't want anything to feel as surfaced
as the conversations she could practically recite in her head.
How was she doing?
She didn't expect the fantasies
of the sunny, green backyards, building life and building love.
How was she breathing?
She didn't care for the long nights,
the terrifying dreams that twisted to pleasant nightmares.
How was she mindful?
She kept it all tucked away behind her ear
with the flowery headbands and innocent daydreams.
How was she okay?
- s.j.l.

Thank you for the stories.
Thank you for being my best friend.
Thank you for the inspiration
in your eagerness to help others.
Thank you for reminding me
that a job isn't a job
if it's something you love.

        Thank you for bringing me a plate of fruit
        every morning.
        Thank you for filling my life
        with books and movies
        and music and dogs.
        Thank you for letting me eat
        the raw dough from the batter.
        Thank you for making my birthday
        a true celebration every year.

Through all of the gratitude
I wish you could see
how much of you
is now part of me.

Thank you, mom.
- s.j.l.

She was a force of nature.
In the quite literal sense, too.
She would push the heaviest of boulders
and move the tallest of mountains.
Armies of crashing waves would wash
over her feet in the sand.
Fields of grass would sway her
as she ran through their vast immensity.
Tree blossoms of pearls would bloom
as she watched from beneath their shadows.
As if her soul was trimmed with gold.
She was a force of nature.
- s.j.l.

Maybe all of those nights spent looking up at the stars together were just foreshadowing how far you'd be from me soon enough, yet always under the same sky.
- s.j.l.

My father would always tell me,
"feed your soul,"
whether it be with
words, art, photographs,
or the effortless observance of nature.

He would then say,
"always have a book,"
whether it be in
a crowded subway, a simple coffeehouse,
an eager airplane ride, or a comfortable couch.

He would yell,
"progress forward,"
whether it be with
dignity, confidence, exhilaration,
or utter despair.

These small pieces of wisdom
he only ever saw as humorous adages
of his inner thoughts
always echoed a bit further into my mind.
I have fed my soul with poetry,
the book I can always have is mine,
and I am certainly moving forward.

Dad, I wrote a book!
- s.j.l.

THE ADVICE

So when it all feels like it's about to come crashing down
and the walls are caving in
and the floor is turning to quicksand,
I need you to tell yourself this.
There have been better days,
and there will be better days.
If this feels like the worst it's been,
let yourself believe that it will be.
Promise yourself
that you won't give in
to the toxicity of his heart anymore.
Bring yourself
to a place inside of your head
that gives you the smallest piece of peace.
Remind yourself
of the times when he made you feel loved and cherished.
Remind yourself
that isn't who he is anymore.
Remind yourself
why you did it all in the first place.
Remind yourself
that it was all for you.

You were sick and tired
of feeling helpless and unwanted.
You deserve your great love story,
your happiest days,
a floor unlike quicksand
and more like a wave coming over your toes.
See the horizon?
That's how far away the bad thoughts will be
as soon as you allow yourself
to believe
that this will be the worst of it.
That the falling and breaking will stop here
and it will stop now.
- s.j.l.

The heartache will teach you
The pain will heal you
The smiles remind you
Nothing can be
here to stay.

The lies will nudge you
The sorrows complete you
The laughing can hold you
against worlds with
patches of gray.
- s.j.l.

Don't you remember a game called connect the dots
when graceful images
emerge
from small points on the paper
don't you see the resemblance in what we do now
as we sit on the grass
connecting the dots in the sky
if only the lessons we learned as kids
to go one by one
could concern us now
but instead
we take it in
all at once.
- s.j.l.

Rebuilding yourself seems easy when you can't exactly
spot your own identity.
The flowers in your garden have grown and grown,
but new seeds can also plant themselves.
There is nothing more beautiful than a new flower,
growing exactly where it wasn't supposed to.
And everyone watches, everyone steps back to see the glow,
the unexpectedness, and the overwhelming relief.
Another piece of your jumbled puzzle, they may say.
Those fantasies of the perfect rows and columns,
color-coordinated daisies and sunflowers illuminating a clear path,
simply unrealistic.

The new ones taking the place of others can't see it,
but you can.
You can feel it, too.
You're growing taller, higher, and stronger
with every heartache, epiphany, and simple day.
Deep breaths,
the path may not be illuminated,
but it's there.
- s.j.l.

I have found myself wishing
for the salt of my tears
to do some of their healing
on the imperfections
of my face.

Maybe
the energy behind my eyes
could stay a bit longer
even though it was
your favorite thing about me.

Maybe
the way my nose moves
when I squint my eyes
could bring someone else a smile
even though
it made you laugh.

Maybe
these aren't imperfections
and maybe
I am okay with them
reminding me of you
and maybe
the salt of my tears
isn't supposed to heal
rather,
fetch me my strength.
- s.j.l.

You learn to fly when you are falling
you learn to swim when you are sinking
so why can't I learn
that because they've come back
means they left in the first place?
- s.j.l.

Walk with me to the edge of the rocks,
swim with me off the end of the docks.
Watch with me as the trains pass us by,
listen with me for planes in the sky.

Sit with me next to the ocean as we hear the waves crash,
listen with me in silence while we watch lightning flash.
Keep still with me as we stare into the vastness of this place,
walk away with me as we leave not but a trace.
- s.j.l.

When pieces of your energy are thrown into the wind, remember this.
Remember that every cloud will blind the fact that the sun and moon will always rise again.
Keep your eyes wide.
Keep your imagination handy.
Inhale, exhale.
Inhale, exhale.
Remember that not all weeds are meant to be pulled out from under the ground.
Remember that the people you choose to surround yourself with
are the people who will shine down on you.
In a week
or a month
or a year,
these people will change.

Remember that time is fleeting yet lasting forever all at once.
Take what you can from that.
Inhale, exhale.
Inhale, exhale.
Leave every piece that makes you feel a bit heavier behind you in the dust.
Keep your eyes wide, forward, and excited.
Don't let those who are temporary destroy your permanence.
Feeling any lighter?
Let yourself float above any sense of anxiety.
Easier said than done, I know.
Let it be, let it grow.
Let it breathe, let it go.
- s.j.l.

People can turn out to be disappointments.
You, my friend, are not.
The memories will be different this time.
Don't give it a second thought.

You are unique in your shadows,
you are willful in your ways.
You are talented and poised,
it will get you down some days.

Remember those that blind us
are only there to stay.
Remember those that love you
are never going away.

Advice for my brother
- s.j.l.

Do you believe in magic
because I do
and I have seen it
work its wonders
in the smallest of ways.
- s.j.l.

Try to tell yourself that everything is leading you
in the right direction.
As if the street signs and forks in the road
tell you any differently.
Every choice is the right path.
Tell yourself this until you feel the least bit lighter.
Nothing about the faint word of experience
is familiar anymore.
Nothing about the drowned out
therapy sessions with your mom
could prepare you
for anything else down the winding road.
Try to bring yourself to a sense of clarity
that allows every old experience to remain new.

Something about the word "familiar" seems
the least bit comfortable.
Something about the thought of it all
makes you never wish to relive anything like it
ever again.
But this should be a reflection.
Those deep belly laughs should be about
new things now,
those long plane rides to new places,
with new people.
Let it be familiar,
but let it also ring in discomfort.
- s.j.l.

Please be gracious with every single step.
Keep yourself held up, keep your chin high.
People are going to prove themselves as self-directed
time and time again,
but you've seen miles past their insecurities.
You've just quite brought yourself to this place of tranquility.
Seeing through their fogged-up lenses
to a place that's a bit more real.
Let them have the satisfaction, for it will help you grow.

For me, a year ago
- s.j.l.

You need to tell yourself that you are seen.
By those mighty large images of self expression in your head.
By those horribly terrifying normals
that have pushed their way past the old fantasies.
By those empathetic, peaceful memories
that aren't only there to tell you that they're over now.
They all see you, and they all hear you.
They understand you like nothing else ever has.
They see you among the peaks and valleys
of the fragments you've always called your growth.
- s.j.l.

How can we get stronger from our own pain?
Taking bites out of the heavy fruit of our souls
seems like the right idea.
And if we still feel malnourished of its bliss,
we would keep on exhausting it
until we feel the least bit full.
- s.j.l.

You have seen people at their worst
and you have wallowed in it yourself.
You cannot let those jet black skies
be the excuse for your drifting.
There is always light.
And if you have somehow managed to drive it all away,
look up at the stars.
They will guide you, always.
You have pushed yourself into these hollow caverns
for much too long.
Didn't anyone ever tell you
that lights are meant to shine?
- s.j.l.

From the dust
you could pick up
gratitude.
From the people
who never found good use for it
anyway.
- s.j.l.

Whoever needs to hear this,
you are allowed to do away with
those that do not serve you.
You are built with so much water inside
so that you can stay afloat
when it becomes
impossible
to stand on two feet
and immersion
seems like a good idea.
- s.j.l.

Don't birds use their wings to fly?
And you let him hang on.
You let him believe
that he was soaring
through the sky
attached right to your own wings.
But the weight got to be too much.
He can't be your project anymore.
You have no obligation
to fix his broken wings.
And even if you did,
even if you thought you did before,
a bird with broken wings can't fly,
even with some help.
Prioritize yourself now.
Fly stronger,
fly faster,
fly higher.

Bring yourself to a place
you've never been before.
Discover things about the world
that you've never seen.
And if you look down a few times
to find him sitting in a tree,
still unable to fly,
I want you to keep moving forward.
The thought of helping him
all over again
will slowly but surely dissolve from your mind
a little more every day.
Believe this for me.
Take it as you will,
take it as you can.
Read it over again.
Feel lighter.
- s.j.l.

Everything changes.
Every door closes, and every other door could be opened.
If something feels like the end of the world, it won't be.
It will be over soon.
The good times, and the bad ones, too.
Nothing is permanent and no one will be there forever.
As scary as it might seem, it could be liberating, too.
- s.j.l.

The stars call your name
as it echoes across the sky
and then straight down to the pavement.
You can hear it this time,
but it rings a bit differently.
It chimes like bells
in your imaginary clock tower,
with strength and with might.
You can feel the strength this time,
but it feels a bit different.
It feels as though it could be mistaken for a part of you.
And please just trust it.
It feels like a part of you
because it is.
- s.j.l.

Walking through a garden seems easy
until you catch sight of the beauty.
And when those flowers seem to have found
their place
right beneath your feet
and you can't help but drown
in bitter despair,
you can practically feel the bliss
slowly replacing
the sorrow.
Like an eager weed
shoving its way to the surface.
And when you've found this sense of
acceptance
within yourself,
I want you to study its every move.
- s.j.l.

And from the splashes of generosity
into the ocean of others
and the mirrors of yourself
on people you never thought you'd affect
take with you the discomfort of it all.
Immerse yourself in the unknown
and jump into the ocean
with them.
- s.j.l.

There's something about the idea
of putting your happiness before everyone else's
that makes it all okay.
And if all of the stars in the sky aren't shining bright
as you stare up through the world,
there's something reassuring
about reminding yourself of your happiness.
And those who come right after
on your list of stars
deserve to shine next to the moon.
It's always changing but my gosh,
your sky will never be more beautiful.
- s.j.l.

You are a bit stronger now, and you're a bit more powerful. You have found that maybe not everyone can feel the things you feel, or maybe they can. You can feel lighter now, and you can sense that the heaviness on your shoulders can find a place to rest. Whether it be the mourning of love, people, or simple friendships, know that others have felt it all the same. Our sameness is also what makes us all so extraordinary.

You are a bit more extraordinary now, and you're starting to feel it within yourself too. Maybe you'll look up at the sky a bit differently, or you'll stare at the flowers in your garden like you can be one with them. Although our paths are different, they can be parallel. I have learned that rejections can be triumphs, and losses can be gains. I have learned that wounds should be covered with band-aids, but you should not hide them. They are too beautiful to be hidden from the world. I have learned that the art of expression is more than words on paper. It is growth, it is comfort, and it is home. You have taught me that. Thank you.
- s.j.l.

Lightning Source UK Ltd.
Milton Keynes UK
UKHW021015210820
368606UK00012B/1054